Collection of poems

Cheryl Reynolds
Collection of poems

Published by Spines
ISBN: 979-8-89569-658-3

Collection of poems

CHERYL REYNOLDS

Contents

Holding One Accountable

JUNE 2, 2003

You must hold those who are in charge
To a higher standard when carrying out
Tasks which are large
They may be human like the rest of us
We will assist them as we prepare and travel by bus

We have a task to assist as long as they carry out
Their duties according to the law
We will carry out every task which is not forbidden
By law
There are many whose task it is to assist along the way
We must stay on track without going astray

Tragically many will fall short of what we expect

They will fall in disgrace losing all respect
Hopefully they have committed no crime
If so they must prepare for a sentence and serve time

Those in high places are not above the law
They are clearly headed for what they truly saw
They shall be brought to justice like the rest
Of us
We are ready to carry it out without a great
Fuss

We clearly say the position to which you were elected
Which Is one we greatly respect
Your disgrace and sin is a shame
Once you are removed things won't be
The same

We seek those who demand high respect
Your position is one in which you must carry out tasks
we respect
Your acts have led to a tragic fall
As a result we will file papers to have you recalled

. . .

Your case will then be sent to the court

There are documents which we will sort

If prosecution is justified then it should be

Carried out

We will then assist them which no one can doubt

IN CONCLUSION I SAY:

Those in high positions will be held to high standards which we all truly respect

They will execute tasks and not fall short

Of what the public expects

If you have a problem with your duties to perform

You should not seek reelection this is a chance for reform

Influenced By Circumstances

JUNE 1, 2001

Many are influenced by what they see
The decisions they Make are those with which
We can't agree
They believe the news they see is good
They try to repeat the acts if they could

They are frequently insensitive and weak
Those who influence them will pursue every
Opportunity they can seek
They are aware of those who are mentally weak
We urge them to reconsider what they seek

Their acts may lead to a life of crime
Because of the suspects state of mind they

Will serve no time
We must seek to prevent acts which all anticipate
Someone must act today, tomorrow will
Be too late

We must establish institutions where the weak
Will get the help they need
This is a call for you to carry out the deeds
We will stop them before they commit a crime
Many will serve to prevent them from serving time

This is a time to seek a decrease in crime
We can't think of a better way for one to carry out
a call
In a matter of time
Depending on their condition, the weak are well
Aware of what they do
Many hope to get by and deceive you

Free speech may not allow us to prevent evil
as we desire
We hope to influence many with the
opportunities they desire

This Will hopefully lead them to change
their way
And seek a better life each and every day

We will assist you in every change you seek
We ask that you don't procrastinate until next
week
This call involves a technical challenge
It is however is not beyond what you can
manage

IN CONCLUSION I SAY:

Any Act which we carry out can influence the
Weak
There are better opportunities for all to seek
Too many are misled and confused
Won't you agree that is an act of psychological
abuse

Innocence Lost Because Of Betrayal

JAN 24, 2013

When my life first began I had no problem with
which I could not cope
I enjoyed prosperity and a future full of hope
All of my needs were fully met
I enjoyed a life full of promises and rich goals set

I was approached by an evil spirit to whom I
foolishly Gave in
I began to lose that perfect resource from within
I must now deal with troubles which did not appear
from The start
How will I cope with these technical matters and not
come Up short

. . .

I was cautioned by my creator and maker informing
Me that I had only one chance
While in that perfect state I was ready to advance
If you fail by the wayside due to a terrible mistake
You make
The suffering down the road is great which you
Will take

I truly dread and regret what I face ahead
If I had the option I would choose a new birth
instead
One mistake caused me terrible suffering in this life
I will seek what I can without strife

I caution my friends not to make the mistake I have
Made
I hope they take notice of the choice I Made
Which is to seek a new chance with the creator who
Understands

I hope you use wise judgment according to his
command

. . .

I would like to see someone who is innocent
gain the Life which was meant for me
I would love to see that day which is a great
Opportunity for all to see
You have the talent to aim and not go astray
Don't repeat my mistake which just isn't the way

I was approached by the enemy of one who gave
Me a chance
By foolishly giving into it slowed or destroyed
My plan to advance
Mankind has not been able to benefit as he should
Because my transgressions prevented me from
Doing what I could

I once had a great opportunity to advance
But through transgression I lost the chance
I must deal with the grief, pain and sorrow
Wondering if there is any hope for tomorrow

I deal with the consequences of the fact
Let this caution you on how to act
I am stressed out because of my sins

But it is not too late for a chance from within

I can seek a new beginning on any given day
As long as I seek a new life I am well on my way
To a new beginning full of challenges and hope
Once I achieve this I look forward to a future
Full of courage, and a chance with which to cope

IN CONCLUSION I SAY:

I strongly urge you not to repeat my sins
The Lord will not put up with such deviant acts
again

Investigate Before You Trust

FEB 21, 2000

You allege you are the one God has sent
With my understanding I know what you meant
I have not had the benefit I should have expected
How do you look for honor and respect

I know without a doubt I am not in the wrong place
I realize my mistake and this is a fact I must face
Let us proceed to make a fresh start
The wok we begun isn't so good, the wise move is for us to depart

The challenges of your post demand a test
The occupant has the burden to bring out the best
Those who rely on you should assist in the tasks
Out of faimess what more can you ask

. . .

No one has demanded more than what you can perform

There is no wisdom in your suggestion that we should not reform

We have suffered long in the past

We have a right to demand a job well done because it will last

Mankind will not prosper with a leader who

procrastinates on

Matters to be managed

There are tasks to be carried out which is a challenge

The time has arrived to procrastinate no more

We face a challenge which demands more courage than before

We have a great challenge not o repeat mistakes which happened in the past

Challenges which are carried out today will result in benefits which

Will last

The outcome from our tasks is expected to benefit all

We must put the right one in charge to carry out this urgent call

Our tasks will no doubt influence those who

depend on us

Which is the main reason they have every

reason to place their Trust

The one who comes forth and answer the call

Will face great challenges to benefit many for

once and for all

We expect every tasks carried out by you to create opportunities giving

All a chance

To carry out calls of their on which will provide an opportunity-

For all to advance

We all know the burdens of our challenges are great

We are ready to procecd before it will be too late

We are seeking ways to expand

We will carry out tasks in demand

Which is a great start for all seeking

opportunities to advance

The only thing we all need is a fair chance

You have been giving that great chance

The challenges you carry out truly give all a

chance to succeed

And advance

Let us faithfully carry out the calls to benefit mankind without delay

He deserves the help he seeks and thank God each and every day

IN CONCLUSION I SAY:

You have problems to address

Those who rely on you should not be burdened with stress

We all believe the person in your post deserves honor and respect

But I ask you have they received the great benefit which they have the right to expect

Is Your Call A Challenge

FEB 2, 2004

Your call should be a challenge
There are tasks which you can manage
You have the talent to fulfill many needs
You will need assistance in carrying out the deeds

Many needed the help they could not find
This may be your call if you don't mind
We are determined that no one will be neglected
Be careful in any task which you have selected

There should be a call for everyone
We will not neglect anyone under the sun
We have been consulted by more than whom
We can handle alone

Some have tried this and things have
Went terribly wrong

We need a few who are dedicated to carrying
Out every task
We will need the assistance of many whom we will
ask
Can we rely on you today
With your help we will proceed without delay

Many have answered their call
They desire to carry out tasks for the benefit
Of all
We regret we don't have too much to
Give
Due to our crisis and the times in which
We live

We must be determined to overcome
So that we can fulfill needs and then some
The time for your benefits are soon
You may not have to wait a minute
Past noon

. . .

We are determined to benefit many beyond a doubt
Is your call one we can rely on to be carried out
We do not expect you to set a call beyond what
You can do
We realize there are limits on any call to bring us
through

IN CONCLUSION I SAY:

Every call should be a challenge
But not beyond what one can manage
We ask that you do your part
There is no better time than today
For all to seek a new start

Life Is A Precious Gift To All

FEB 13 2000

The time we have on Earth is the gift of life
We must cease from all envy madness and strife

What other gift is there so precious and dear
We must live life to the fullest without fear

We must make good use of our time or suffer a setback
We all work to eliminate calamities which lead us of track
There is a time for everything we experience

Once we exercise the freedom we will notice we all make
Such a great difference

We have a lot to give an account of while we seek a challenge

We must set the priorities straight with challenges so we can Manage

You must seek, that precious gift you were brought to perform

Once the task is completed we are ready to proceed with

Order and reform

Life is too short for confusion on any day

You must eliminate all disasters or risk losing everything

To be enjoyed along the way .

There are many who are desperate to benefit from what

You can give

Once they receive it they can seek a better life to live

I thought you were chosen to carry out the gift you were

Given at birth

There are too many people who are suffering right here on earth

They have waited long enough for a chance to produce and create

We can no longer tolerate one who waste time or procrastinate

We demand that a leader come forth today and the time is now

We have one question to ask which is to show us how

To carry out our tasks and benefit mankind while we still

Have a chance

We wish him well in his tasks

And joyfully witness as he advances

We all have a life which will tell a story

Whatever it says and is a blessing to many we can

All say to God be the glory

We desire to create a chance for you tomorrow

This is the first step to bringing an to all sorrow

If you forgot the lessons we learned in the past

The present should teach how to focus on

Things which last

I thought 1 carried out several challenges which many said they will follow through

The tasks are too many for them alone we have discovered someone is missing, is it you

you are the cause we have not had the chance to start on time

Those who relied on us are suffering and tumed into a life of crime now that they have been tried convicted and landed in jail

We deeply regret the lives of many were wasted and all plans felled

We have a chance to reform those which are lost we have to suffer and sacrifice with compassion at such a great cost

The soul which we save has something to give

The performance of great talent with the will to live

IN CONCLUSION I SAY:

. . .

Time is short seek every chance to perform give and live what a great gift from the one he or she has to give

Remember we have only a short time here on Earth 50 let us use it for the benefit of all

There is no greater gift than

hope for all

Lonely Tasks

JUNE 18, 2012

You face a great task when you are alone
Be careful or serious matters will go wrong
There are many who will assist in many tasks
They are available whenever you ask

The tasks are many which you will face
Why not seek assistants who are ready to take their
place
They are well qualified for the positions they seek
Why not fulfill them and get started this week

They are ready to join and participate
They will correct any problem which one can
Anticipate

They will not procrastinate
You should consider them before its too late

They have sought to carry out a great call
Many have been located down the hall
Are any tasks available for them to carry out
Why not give them the benefit of a doubt

Many needs will be fulfilled by their experience
They have been successful and have made a
Difference
You will not have time to fulfill all tasks
Many are knocking at the door waiting to be asked

We know our experience can benefit you today
You and those you serve will suffer if there is a
delay

You have the opportunity to ease suffering
when its needed the most
Until the task is completed none will leave
their post
We repeat the task is too heavy for you

to carry out alone
Thank God nothing has gone wrong
You must seek help while you can
We share your concern and truly
understand

IN CONCLUSION I SAY:

This is an opportunity
which may no longer be found
You should bave taken advantage of it
when assistants where around
You have neglected
Opportunities you should have sought
Yesterday

Many have fulfilled those tasks today

Love And Discipline A Perfect Match

JAN 8, 2008

We must answer a call and perform tasks which
are mighty tough
In our journey, we face burdens which are
mighty rough
We must not fall short of what is expected
Neither will we fall into situations which are
disrespected

Love is a difficult task which we must all
endure
Discipline requires that you have a task which
you must assure
We have all experienced that love is not an -casy
task

Discipline on the other hand requires tough
tasks which are expected to last

True love demands that we be sensitive of those
for whom we care
Discipline demands that we be considerate
thoughtful and ready to share
Love instructs us to reach for higher standards
from a greater source
Discipline demands a follow up on from a
standard of a higher source

Love is not selfish but full of acts so kind
Discipline instructs us to be humble and sincere
if we don't mind
We all desire the best which love has to offer
Discipline is a demand that we be generous in
all that we give

You believe you love as you should
Does self-discipline Icad you to do the best that
you could ?
An act of love is not seeking your own way ,

Self-discipline calls for your best each and
every day

Love will surely change the way you give
Self-discipline will rule over how you should
live
Love is a way which isn't blind
By self-discipline you will be kind

Love is a gift which generated from above
Self-discipline is an example of true love
Love is a gift which is hard to match
Self-discipline throws out hints for you to catch

Love is a remedy from which problems are
solved
Discipline leads the way for you to get involved
When you love. You will lead, guide, train and
encourage
Self-discipline is hard to follow yet it leads the
way to never get discouraged

Love is patient long suffering and endures a lot

Self-discipline demands tolerance, being
considerate.
And living a life which says a lot
Love will challenge you some day
You will have a task to fulfill without delay

IN CONCLUSION, I SAY:

Mankind is seeking the talent for the acts you
have performed
Self-discipline require that you prepare, get
organized, and seek Opportunities for reform
Mankind is asking that you join him and lead the
way
Self-discipline will prepare you to get involved
and make a difference today

Mankind Must Be Saved

JAN 5, 2001

We, the agents of mankind are tired of procrastination
We seek high standards and demand participation
We have many needs to fulfill
And until they are all met we will never sit or stand
still

We know many are truly reliable and seek positions
Today
We will maintain high standards and carry out tasks
without
Delay
There is a space for you to carry out your task
Sticking to high standards is a command for which we
ask

. . .

We must set standards for all who answer their
Call
They have the talent to benefit us all
They will need help along the way
Let us do what we can to save the day

The standards we set are laws by which you
Must abido
We will not tolerate sub standards as we have decided
If you cannot live up to the demands and comply
It is time to search for another place to
Perform your task. Goodbye

By carrying out your task, many will hopefully
Get their desire
Once they are satisfied, they are the ones who you
Will inspire
There is no demand higher than ours to save mankind
From the trouble he face any day
We shall set higher standards along the way
We will not be satisfied until all are satisfied and well
We will not rest until this is achieved when only

Time will tell

Let what you have read serve you for the
rest of
Your life
You may handle daily trouble without strife
You have suffered a lot and have overcame
A lot of pain
Now that you are well you have a lot to gain

You must take time use care and be truly fair
As you live your doubts troubles and fears
Will be rare
You have high hopes which lead to goals to
achieve
Proceed use care and in time you will thank
God for
What you receive

We all have a duty to serve man
We must strive to do what we can
We all have a tougl task which-will-
Come to past

The benefit from this task will last

You are called to carry out a task in demand
Your talent stresses the facts stating a
command
We all have serious needs
you have the ability to carry out the deed

IN CONCLUSION IN ISAY:

Mankind seeks to prosper for a better life
You must carry out your tasks without strife
Mankind will suffer no more once he has
found you
He desires a task for you to carry out
which will
Bring him through

Mankinds Remedy Against Social Injustice

JUNE 2, 2000

We face injustice each and every day
We will seek every remedy without delay
We are engaged in a tough fight
Which will result in what we know is right

We will seek justice without delay
We will carry out the tasks which starts today
There is a lot of help which we will seek
Many of the tasks will start this week

Many will be arrested and whom the system will
try
They will be found innocent which no one can
deny

Then are not guilty of any crime
Their arrest was only a waste of time

We cannot always trust the law
It frequently results in favoritism which we saw
The greatest defense was based on race
This is a denial of justice which should not have
taken place

Justice is a remedy for which many have fought
There are remodies which many have sought
There is a remedy which we will carry out
Everyone will be given the benefit of a doubt

We will seek these remedies as we head for
court
We must set aside differences of every sort
We need your assistance without delay
The tasks which are assigned to you must be
Carried out no later than today
We will seek an opportunity for tomorrow
Many will benefit leaving no room for sorrow
We urge you to seek every opportunity you can

get

You must make sure your priority is set

IN CONCLUSION I SAY:

Justice is a task worth fighting for

Many will benefit and suffer no more

The tasks will be carried out by only a few

We can only wonder if one of them is reserved

for you

Mankind Seeks a Change: Is This Your Opportunity

JUNE 11, 2004

Mankind faces a crisis which demand a change

We face situations which we took time to

Arrange

This is an opportunity for all to get involved

Can you assist us in the problems to be solved ?

We sought help which we could not find

This is a call for you if you don't mind

Can we rely on you today?

We have to act without unnecessary delay

The crisis-we-face-are mighty-great

We must act this moment because tomorrow

Will be too late

The crisis should have been solved in the past
We had no idea who we could rely on until we
Found you at last

Many missed the opportunity they should
Have sought yesterday
This will multiply the problems which
Must be solved today
This is a call for you to seek
Which should be carried out by next week

Mankind will be better off tomorrow
If many tasks are carried out leaving no room
For sorrow
There must be priorities for all to set
Which involves tough standards already
met

We have all suffered grief in the past
This is a day for hope which we pray
Will last
We will sacrifice when crisis are at hand
We will have no choice but will be

Expected to meet tough demands

You will have to fulfill a task which is mighty large
You will need assistance from those who you
Put in charge
The task is too large for you to carry out alone
You have tried this before which resulted in things
Going terribly wrong
IN CONCLUSION I SAY:

Mankind will seek benefits
benefits which no one
Will doubt he deserves
Calls must be carried out in
which many will serve
we urge all to take their place
while there is time
Our budget is short and we will
Down to the last dime

Mankind Suffers From Confusion And Misunderstanding

JAN 1, 2005

We are frequently faced with problems
Which no one understands
This is a task in which to take
Difficult commands
Many try to understand but
End up confused
We must put our resources to
Good use

We must seek opportunities which all
Understand
This will ease a problem-at hand
Many were taught but ended up
Confused

Hopefully no one was a victim of
Neglect or abuse

This is a challenge which is tough
The task must be carried out
Which is tough
We hope it is one you truly understand
You will be able to carry out the task
At hand

We tried to show many the way
They didn't understand and ruined
Our day
This is a problem we must correct
Many were misled and were truly
Upset

A lack of understanding won't accomplish
Very much
As a result there are many who are truly out
Of touch
Confusion which is present today
Has led to a mess

This is a great disaster which we
Must confess

A lack of understanding won't
Give anyone the benefit of a doubt
With this being true a lot of calls will not be
Carried out
We seek understanding in what we need
We may end up back on track and fulfill

Many needs

How did such a misunderstanding
Result in the first place
Someone was negligent and did not
provide reasonable space
We will be carful in whom we seek
This is too important to procrastinate
Until next week

IN CONCLUSION I SAY:

We all have a task which we must

understand

If you don't please step aside which

a great demand

We will eliminate any misunderstanding

of the past

otherwise there will be difficulty in

Raising hope and opportunities at

last

News: How Does It Affect Us

FEBRUARY 1, 2004

We frequently hear events which are new
We are only familiar with a few
Any event may change which we see and do
How will any event influence anyone
performed by you

News which we frequently hear is what we
don't Expect
Several are gross resulting in disrespect
We often have no idea of what is to come
We do however wonder where many events
started from

. . .

Have you heard anything new
What I did not expect is such a reaction from
you
You have probably never heard of that before
The same event occurs every day on another
floor

News will affect you as long as you survive
Similar events happen to everyone while alive
Just be careful of how news influence you
Those who aren't influence are only very few

One critical influence of news reflects in ones
Mental health
Others are influenced by positive results
resulting
In prosperity and wealth
Some news is what you can't get around
At times news is present wherever it is found

If you watched the news last night
Those reporting it have a schedule
which is tight

I thought I would discover what
1 have never seen before
The news I saw was the same
which was reported on the floor

News are events which keep us
up to date
We must take notice before it's
too late
When it is present take time to
observe
Those who report it have
answered
their call to serve

IN CONCLUSION I SAY:

The news you watch will
influence you in some way
your tasks may influence
many every day
News is what you see as long
as you are alive

How it influence you will

determine how you survive

Suffering Due To Conflict

JUNE 1, 2003

You will run into conflict in whatever you do

Show respect and give credit to whom it is due

Many will have a different point of view

If you listen you will discover something which

Is new

You can't expect everyone to see things

Your way

They may discover something new each and every day

They should be given the benefit of a doubt

They may have a plan which probably should be

Carried out

. . .

Everyone probably won't benefit the same way
However let them enjoy it without delay
It just may lead to reconciling our differences
We can't hope for a better experience

Somcone may try to solve a problem which 9
Many truly don't understand
This is when many truly insist on they own way
Which they truly demand
This attitude is not good from the start
It is a waste of time which is short

The task you seek may be carried out in various
Ways
Someone's point of view may be different from
Yours any day
We seek to eliminate all conflicts of view
And will truly give credit to whom it is due

IN CONCLUSION I SAY:

We are anxious to hear your point of
View

We are always open to any point which may

Be new

We will assist you in any way we can

We expect every task to be carried out which is

In demand

Stay Clear Of Harm

JUNE 2, 2003

You will be approached by many who are
not what they appear to be
They are out to deceive which only a
few can see
You should observe all who are around
The one meaning good is not easily found

Their motives are secret and not easily
observed
They have only evil intentions which no one
deserves
When approached as questions regarding
what
They may desire

Be suspicious the one you question just may
be a liar

They seek to avoid who they believe is
smart
The weak is their priority while time is
Short
They try to convince you, knowing
You are not informed
What they seek to avoid is a task leading
To reform

We will proceed against any crime which
they
Seek to carry out
Our first priority is to seek justice which no
One can doubt
If you are a witness to any act which is
Contrary to what is right
We need your assistance while we protect,
Defend and fight

The crook knows they will run out of luck

Someday

The first step is to put them out of business

Starting today

They will seek a place where they feel safe

And hide

They know we will deal with their victims

In whom we confide

They will be located down the street

What they fear is the day we will meet

They will be brought to justice one day

Which will certainly be carried followed

Without delay

The victims will be compensated for what

They went through

To the crook:

We have a tough message for you

We regret what your victim experienced

Yesterday

How about you facing justice without delay

IN CONCLUSION I SAY:

. . .

If you carry out an act contrary to the Law
We have witnesses who testify against you
Regarding any matter they saw
You will face justice with a sword
Be aware: As we approach you we have
A mighty tough word

Suffering A True Teacher

JUNE 6, 2004

We regret that many are suffering which they
Don't deserve
This is a task in which many will serve
The task is difficult to carry out
Many will benefit which no one can doubt

Many have suffered from mistakes from their
Past
These mistakes should not ruin their future which
Has arrived at last
They should be given another chance
To prosper succeed and advance

We will seek a chance for them to succeed

They will be given every opportunity in deed
They will seek your assistance along the way
Hopefully they will land on their fect someday

They have learned from their mistakes
Can you assist in the choice they make
They sought assistance which could not
Be found
They finally ran into you who was
Always around

Those who suffered from mistakes they made
Truly believe that justice was carried out and not
Delayed
They believe they have suffered enough
They have accepted the consequences which
Were tough

Suffering may be consequences for doing wrong
Justice was carried out before it was too long
Can you assist while the hour is late
Justice was expedited and could not wait

. . .

Those who enforce principles have a task

Which is rough

The task requires decisions which are tough

We have seen many suffer who are walking down the

Street

There is no telling who they will meet

IN CONCLUSION I SAY

Suffering should serve as

Justice for acts which are wrong

some may seek a delay of

justice which is wrong

we will prevent this with a

New task we know that many will assist whenever they are asked

Suffering: It's A Serious Message

JUNE 6, 2004

Suffering is frequently the consequences of choices

we make

This is the time to learn from your mistake

Others may discover what acts to prevent

Or suffer similar consequences in any event

Suffering is an opportunity to make one wise

It is a penalty in action which no one should

despise

There are mistakes which suffering seeks to correct

This is the time to get priorities set

Suffering seeks to make the crooked straight

It will send a message while it is late

Some may get the message before they act
For others it will take a course and reflection
On how society reacts

Suffering is not a choice
It however is a loud and clear voice
Suffering is a task all alone
It will correct you when your choice is wrong

Suffering demands a lot of time
It may serve as a penalty for a crime
You will miss out on what we already know
You have acted contrary to the way you should go

There are opportunities you will surely miss
Your family may suffer from not receiving
A kiss
Your family will miss not having you around
They will see you where you can easily be found
You will be relieved from suffering
one day
you should prepare for another way
opportunities will be hard to find

someone will truly assist you which
they truly don't mind

IN CONCLUSION I SAY:

Suffering demands a lot of time
it may be the result of your crime
you may be relieved once you are out
the life you seek will determine if you are
given the benefit of a doubt

Tasks In Demand

JUNE 18 2012

There are tasks which are in great demand
Which is beyond what many can understand
The task is one for which you have the talent
Talent is a message which God has sent

There is a challenge which must be carried out
All may benefit which no one can doubt
The challenge should be fulfilled without delay
Which will benefit us all without delay

Fulfilling your challenge will fulfill needs while it is day
Many will rise to their feet and be shown the way
They desire to carry out a great call
Who can benefit from their challenge which isn't small

. . .

People we recruited weren't able to fulfill their tasks
They ran into misfortune seeking relief for which they asked
You will take on their task
Performing your best which is all we ask

We regret many were neglected when those we
Recruited failed to carry out their challenge
Perhaps it was one which they could not manage
We had to replace them without delay
Tomorrow is a challenge in which they will benefit
Any day

We must review a task which one carries out
The servants will be given different routes
Those we seek to benefit reside in multiple
Locations
We will try to assist you in any given situation

We must be sensitive to many situations we face
As we start the task we ask that all take their place
There were challenges which were overlooked
Many challenges of your task require a second look

. . .

IN CONCLUSION I SAY:

Today is the day to carry out your
challenge
We Know it is one which you can
certainly manage
If you need assistance never fail to ask
It is an obligation of many in carrying
out their tasks

Taking The Law Into Your Own Hands

JUNE 23, 2002

The law should be clear for all to
Understand
Everyone should abide by it which is
A great command
We urge you to be careful and
Not go astray
Or you will quickly be brought to justice
Without delay

We will provide protection for the
Benefit of all
Those who carry out justice will
Carry out a tough call
We truly seek your assistance each

And cvery day
We will provide opportunities
With no future delay

The law will seek to fulfill several
Needs
It will seek to prevent corrupt and
Evil deeds
Many who run from trouble whom the
Law is meant to protect
The victim should not suffer while
Waiting for the law to go into effect

Those who enforce the law may not
Always be around
They need laymen who are easily
Found
Are they allowed to take the
Law into their hands
They must be taught and clearly
Understand

There will be consequences which they will face

We urge them to be gentle and stay
In their place
They are free to make a citizen's arrest
They must know what procedures to carry
Out and do their best

IN CONCLUSION I SAY:

The public appreciates their assistants
without delay
we can all feel safe and protected any
day
We will tell the one who goes astray
We will catch up with you any day
And won't be happy until justice is
carried out without delay

The Frustrations Of Mankind

JAN 31, 2004

Mankind has suffered from so much sorrow grief and pain
He is searching for remedies for hope
And happiness from which there is something
To gain
He is motivated to take whatever action is needed without
Delay
How sensitive we all must truly be for a plan which works
Well today

There are a lot of tasks to carry out
Who can we rely on without a doubt
The tasks are too important to leave
To anyone

Our minds will be made up before the day
Is done

The tasks will be carried out to fulfill many needs
Can we rely on you to carry out good deeds
There is so much suffering among many
We must come to their rescue without
Neglecting any

We will make every reasonable sacrifice
Before we do we need to seek sound advice
We will seek advice which is sound
It will be the truth which no one
Can get around

We have sought to case frustration yesterday
Seeking one who is reliable without a delay
We must seek one whose experience can
fulfill our needs
We can truly rely on them to carry out
The deeds

Will you assist us in seeking one to fill

The post
They should be talented which is needed
The most
Will they be available today
We truly wish to proceed without delay

We must fulfill needs which
have been neglected far too
long
Those who went before us
have unfortunately neglected
many tasks far too long
This will create many tasks
which we will face
Today is the day we must
take our place

IN CONCULSION I SAY:

We must deal with frustration to
A certain extent
This is something which we just
can't prevent

how you deal with it is a

challenge

the task is yours in how you

manage

The Tasks For Our Greatest Demand

NOV 25,2015

We have a need which should be carried out
Many should be given the benefit of a doubt
We have truly suffered enough
Whoever carries out the tasks will certainly
Face a challenge which is tough

We regret that many have suffered in the past
Hopefully this burden will not last
You asked that we give you a chance
You have convinced us that through your efforts
We will advance

We will work with you in getting your priorities

Straight

We pray to God it is not too late

Many have overlooked the chance they had

There are consequences which left many hopeless and sad

We shall seek opportunities without delay

This will remove all obstacles in the way

We look forward for you to do your part

As we begin a new day we are ready to start

We will seek to fulfill each and every need

We will proceed to carry out the deed

We must not procrastinate at any time

Many have not Had the chance to earn A dime

We must carry out challenges which were left undone

We truly have a chance which has only just begun

We look forward for many to be blessed

We have neglected them which we must

Truly confess

They will be on feet soon

In the meantime, the task must be completed

Around noon

We have sacrificed and truly made a way

For many to enjoy success each and every day

IN CONCLUSION I SAY:

We will give you the opportunity to

carry out your task

Help is avallable for all who ask

We must not procrastinate along the

way

Otherwise success will be delayed any

day

WE HAVE THE VICTORY THROUGH THE BLOOD OF JESUS

Author: Cheryl Reynolds
Date: Aug 23, 2008

Christ paid the price for our sins
Had it not been for him we will be engaged in a
War we just can't win
There is no name under Heaven by which we can be save
Christ is due all honor under Heaven for the life he gave

It is the desire of God that you prosper and live
And follow his example in how to love and live
He suffers a great deal during his life which he gave
There is no other way by which we can be saved

His ways without doubt will never come up short
If you desire fellowship with him you must surely do your part
He gets no joy when you procrastinate
He is ready for all who will participate

Let us not forget that Christ once for all
If you live the live there are many people to call
The ways of the Lord are full of grace
As a believer this is the time to take your place

Christ has given his life to fulfill our most critical noed
This is a chance to enjoy life with the father in deed
He suffer and died which he did not deserve
This is a moment in history which we truly observe

IN CONCLUSION I SAY:

As believers Christ has truly influenced us by the life we live
He urges us all to be generous in what we give

It is time to commit to him today
until you do you continue in your sins by procrastinating
and going astray

We Will Call On You

AUG 2, 2002

We faced a lot of challenges
From the start
We had to fulfill them while time
Was short
We were referred to many who were
Around
What about you who could not be
Found

Someone located you yesterday
There was a task which remains
Unfulfilled-today
Many have failed in their tasks
What about you is a question

We ask

You have a busy task which will
Soon be carried out
Many will be given the benefit
Of a doubt
Can we rely on you when there
Is a need
We seek those who are willing
To carry out good deeds

We were unfortunate while relying
On those we trusted in the past
They were put in charge of tasks
Taking too long while time passed
Will you be able to make a difference
Today
And carry out the task without delay

There are also many with talent who
Wander around
There are opportunities which remain
To be found

Many of them don't know where to go
We will get the word out so they will
Know

You were sought when we ran into
trouble this year
One rushed to our aid relieving us
from fear
He was given a task to fulfill
He was determined to carry out
God's will

Many have suffered and we have witnessed
this enough
We will recruit many to carry out
Tasks which are rough
Many have referred us to you
They said you have experience
and with your experience the task
Is not new

IN CONCLUSION I SAY:

. . .

There are many who did well in the past

Many have benefited, and this is expected

to last

Those on whom we can rely on are on a few

Should one of the tasks be left for you

We Wont Be Led Astraty

JAN 14, 2001

Many may carry out tasks which aren't relevant to
their call
For many this led to a tragic fall
They seek to get back on track
Which requires resources they lack

They recognize they made a mistake
We are prepared to assist them in whatever actions
they take
You have the talent to assist us along the way
We will begin the task without unnecessary delay

They acted in good faith but were deceived
They sought assistance which they were glad to

receive

Those who walk contrary to what is right

Took advantage of what was in sight

They sought every crooked way they can

When caught they headed for the street down which

They ran

They didn't get very far

We were able to chase them down in your

Car

We witl hold them accountable according to the law

They are the ones whom the witnesses saw

She said they tried to get her involvod

She quickly recognized a problem she can solve

We will go undercover and catch

Whoever we can

We hope to capture them before they

caryout-their plan

Once we get them off the street

We will recognize there are many

needs we will meet

. . .

We strongly urge you to consider
changing your way
There is a better life you should
prepare for today
Getting our way, you will not lead
any astray
If you are caught prepare for
justice any day

IN CONCLUSION I SAY:

We are ready to carry out our tasks
and serve
We will protect the public which
they richly deserve
If we are informed of any crime
Be prepared to do the time.

When Do We Hear And Recognize Our Call

FEB 6, 2000

There is a need for a task to be fulfilled

Among us only a few have the talent and will

We truly suffer day by day because you do not recognize your call

Mankind cannot advance until the job is done for the benefit of all

Everyone has the right to see the benefit he needs

The only remedy is your performance in deed

The tasks of your call are urgent and you must perform

By procrastinating there is no chance for reform

If you recognize a talent which should be carried out and you have the desire

It may well be a call which you richly inspire

Have you searched for a place where there is a need there?

Give it a try and seek to carry out the deed

Have you been approached by one experiencing suffering and sorrow

Maybe this is your chance to carry out a task full of inspiration for

Tomorrow

The tasks you have carried out has a lot of work for the benefit of all

Tomorrow

Don't overlook opportunities which will inspire a lot of people along

The way

They have urgent needs you will see each and evert day every

You have been approached by one who is looking for a way to seek

Life and a chance with which to cope

Can this be your call to inspire one with courage and hope ?

Walk with them as they seek a way

To answer their call each and every day

They are motivated to carry out the tasks making their call

A success

They are generous, eager and seek problems to address

What a great benefit for mankind to enjoy

Isn't this the time for the soul to sing with joy

As we listen for and any day

Let us prepare ourselves as we prepare to fight all the way

For that great challenge, we are so eager to recognize

Once we do we have a great duty to set up and organize

Many will call on us to perform various tasks

All they have to do is seek our help and ask

We stand ready to sacrifice and carry out

Gods will

Until the task is completed we will not

Stand still

As long as our needs remain unfulfilled

is a call for someone to

Recognize

Once we are satisfied this brings them greater honor than what you realize

We are honored as the task is carried out the servant truly has the

Ability without a doubt

. . .

Your call is one from which God will carry out his command

It is a great task which

Comes with great demands

We must recognize those who are ready to carry out their call and

Firmly stand there is a need to search for a plan and truly carry out every demand

When A Friend Goes Astry

JUNE 7, 2004

You have a friend who has gone terribly astray
He conspired against a friend yesterday
You are offended and don't understand
It's time to let go and release
His hand

You have discovered this is a tough time
When you needed him, he didn't have a dime
This should be a lesson regarding those
With whom you trust and associate
You must make the right choice before
It's too late

You may not know the person until an

Event takes place
Keep your distance with limited space
Something will occur before very Iong
Hopefully you won't be a victim when
Things go wrong

While seeking a friend it is better to take
Your time
Otherwise, you may be the victim of a crime
He may not be the right one for you
Those you can rely on are very few

You should proceed and select one mighty
Slow

There is no telling what their colors may
Show
Their colors will truly come out
Everyone agrees with this which.no one
Can doubt

The truth will come out which you can't
Hide

You may conspire which begins inside
Your colors will put you to shame
Your reputation will never be then same

A friend sent from God is hard to find
He will sacrifice and truly
When times are tough you won't be left alone
He will correct a situation before things go wrong

IN CONCLUSION I SAY:

There is one who is right for you
You will find them before the day is through
Have you met the one who is
Right?
They will arrive on time before tonight

Who's Need Will Your Talent Satisfy

MAY 16 2004

We have great desires but before we can fulfill

Them we have needs which must be met

The first task is to set things in order with priorities

Set

There ara calls for only a few

We truly wonder will one of them be you

There were great talents which were carried out

By only a few

Someone saw you yesterday and many asked

What about you

We were told your call last year was great

We truly need you before it's too late

. . .

We need you to carry out a task today
Can we rely on you without delay
You can carry out your task with the assistance
Of many
We will fulfill needs without neglecting any

Have you decided when you are willing to start
We hope it's today whife time is short
Many are suffering today
They seek relief without unnecessary delay

If you are not available just let us know
We will then know the direction in which we
Should go
We are off to a late start
We will not procrastinate while time
Is short

Those who have procrastinated have
Made the task more difficult to carry out
In spite of this we are determined to carry it out
We will seek the assistance while there is a need
Those coming to our rescue are ready to carry out the deeds

. . .

Many have responded to our requests
We will seek whom we know is the best
They are the ones on whom we can rely
When given the task they promptly replied

IN CONCLUSION I SAY:

We have more tasks that what we oan handle
alone
We will proceed without waiting too long
We are seeking your assistance while the hour
Is late
We hope you will join us and not procrastinate

Without a Sacrifice Your Call Will Not Succeed

JAN 3, 2010

You have a call which should be carried out
Many will surely benefit beyond a doubt
One essential obligation is a willing to
Sacrifice
Without a sacrifice we will suffer and pay an
Undesirable price

There is a tough task ahead
There are many who have suffered instead
They expect you to sacrifice what you can
A tragedy will result if you fail to plan

You-should-not carry out the-task-alone
But you insisted and we all see what will go

Terribly wrong
There is a chance as we seck a new start
We must proceed while time is short

Many calls are truly in demand
Our tasks will benefit those who need a heip in hand
Are you available to assist us today
There is a task which should be fulfilled without delay

Many have been successful in the past
Your call should benefit mankind providing
Help at last
He has sought an opportunity to get on his feet
There are demands he has failed to meet

No oue was available when he needed assistance
Yesterday
Your sacrifice can provide relief today
He has a call for the benefit of all
The sacrifice we request is minimum and small

We will assist him until his needs are met
There are time limits which we set

If we desire success we have challenges to meet
Many will assist as they rise on their feet

IN CONCLUSION I SAY:

There are many who seek assistance today
A small sacrifice we seek along the way

Many will benefit as they seek opportunities
along the way
They will prosper and enjoy a lovely day

You Are Honored With A Gift

JAN 5, 2005

We were informed of your gifts talents and ability to reform

You may in fact be the agent we need to lead us to reform

We face a lot of tasks and challenges before us today

We have goals and standards we will set any day

We are ready to take every action the tasks calls for and carry it out

We are faithful confident and ready to carry it out without a doubt

We ask that you give us your time and talent and take time to

Understand

Once you honor this request we are ready to carry out our

Command

You have told us to set our priorities in order and proceed

We have followed this advice and carried out awesome deeds
We have also created jobs which demand that each exercise
Their gifts
Carrying them out without procrastinating and acting mighty
Swift

We can say that we have sought agents in the past
We truly rejoice in the one which we found at last
we know you have what it takes to led the way
we look forward to working with you any day

with your heip none will go astray
they will do well and this will make a way
for all of us to search for higher goals we can achieve
and teach
the first step is to listen to the one who teach

we ask that you teach lead guide and train
once you succeed there is something for all to gain
this will open doors for higher standards for all to seek
while setting our priorities we must stay humble and meek
SAY:

. . .

you must be sensitive to the ones who rely on you today

your response will be critical along the way

many will be affected at a time which no one expects

this tells you that your task must be carried out with all due respect

Our instructors from the past have taught us well and taught us to observe

There is an urgent position we must rely on next year one must carry out the task in the future which is near

mankind will rely on

You to carry out the tasks with care and perform it right as the day comes to a close and we have been blessed we bate to say good night

We have been blessed from the start now is the time to bless others while time is short

with the legacy you leave you have taught many how well they can do they will follow the lead and never fall short of standards set by you

IN CONCLUSION I

You have a gift which we all follow the lead keeping many inspired

Many will seek goals which you have taught

Once they do what a lovely lifetime remains

Which we have all Sought

Your Past How It Reflects You Today

JUNE 2, 2003

Your past is full of events
Many of which you could not prevent
Man looks at one's past to make decisions
Today
Unfortunately, such events should not
Hinder success along the way

Someone may not be given a chance to advance
Due to past events which happened by chance
A person may have no choice in some events
Tragically success is something which someone
Will try to prevent

This is an obstacle which many will face

Someone will assist while there is space
You will be given a chance
To prosper succeed and advance

One may have made tragic mistakes
In the past
A good future just may be around the
Corner at last
Most believe one should be given a
Second chance
They may have the talent to succeed
And advance

We will open the door for many
Seeking to remove all obstacles if any
We can send them on their way
They can then begin a new life
Any day

There are a lot of jobs which must
Be filled
We will carry out the task according
To Gods will

Many positions have been vacated
Far too long
As a result, businesses have failed
And things went terribly wrong

Many weren't given a chance
Which hindered their opportunity to
advance
As we said they made a mistake in
their past
It should not hinder opportunities
For a successful future at last

IN CONCLUSION I SAY:

There is a task in which all should
be allowed to serve
we will give them the chance they
deserve
Their talent will benefit many
As they carry out their task without
Neglecting any

Your Teaching: Who Will It Influence

APRIL 24, 2004

You said you have a call to teach
There are many who your words will
Reach
Many may seek help and be encouraged
Beware of one who goes astray
Will you become despondent and discourage

There are times when we all seek to learn
Those who teach are given respect which they
Must earn
We have learned many things which weren't
Known in the past
We just may discover opportunities at last

. . .

We just may end up in a teaching position
Some day
If this is what we desire, we shall proceed
Without delay
We must not deny any the chance
To learn while they have a chance
This just may be their opportunity to
Succeed and advance

Many who are motivated just do not know where
To go
They tried to find the place which no one knows
We will seek them wherever they can be found
We will need assistance of many who are around

This is the opportunity to seek whoever they can
There are principles which all should understand
The one who teaches has a tough task
Seek the assistants who may be asked

Will you seek the position of a teacher
today
If so, you should seek the task without

delay
The future of those who are taught will
suffer no delay If you are not ready we
ask that you step aside while
It is day

The position of teaching is rough
Numerous tasks are involved which
Are tough
You should seck advice from those you ask
Is this a position for you, if so, proceed to
carry
Out the tasks

IN CONCULSION I SAY:

There are many positions for those seeking
to teach
There are many whom your teachings will
reach
Many are given the opportunity to learn
Once they are through, they will have
Every chance to succeed prosper and earn

You Are Not Challenged Enough

JULY 20, 2008

You are in a position calling for challenges which are mighty tough

The road ahead may be excited but without a doubt it is also one which is

Rough

The nature of your position is to relieve many of stress

When the task Is carried out it is time to Thank God for those who

Are relieved and blessed

You have taken a wise step in answering your call

Now is the time for mankind to benefit for once and for all

Your call involves many challenges for you to carry out

We are very confident you will succeed without a doubt

. . .

Your call also involves challenges giving many a chance to succeed
This is the first step for prosperity indeed
Challenges are a great opportunity which everyone deserves
This is your chance to seek, perform, and serve

Crisis are the result of neglected calls
There is a solution in the call you may have selected
There are challenges for all to get involved
This is the first step for all problems to be solved

Many have been upset and truly depressed
Does your call provide relief for the problems to be addressed
Those who are depressed need relief today
Tomorrow they will be well enough to get on their way

Your call should provide the challenges and opportunities they need
This will truly open many doors indeed
Your call may also offer many a great chance to be blessed
There can be no better opportunity for those suffering from stress

You have an opportunity to serve mankind today
The challenge should be carried out without delay
Crisis also create many opportunities for all to serve mankind

Now that you have a chance, you should do your part if
You don't mind

Depression results when needs aren't carried out
A challenge must be fulfilled for relief which no one can doubt
These challenges should be part of your call
When you fulfill your task, that is a blessing for all

Your Call: Will It Solve Our Crisis

JUNE 18, 2012

Crisis result from calls being neglected
A call was not carried out from one we
selected
We have asked them to seek another way
Which will allow us to proceed without delay

We find no excuse in what many have
Found
Tragic facts are present which no one can get
around
We will seek every opportunity tomorrow
Many will be relieved of heartache, pain and
sorrow

. . .

You can assist in calls which you will
carry out
We will assist you giving you the benefit
of a doubt
We ask for your assistance without delay
Which will truly end crisis each and every day

We seek assistants who we can motivate
They are ready to proceed before it's too late
They have informed us that they will
Proceed as never before
Their performance will influence many
Resulting in open doors

We ask that all proceed and not procrastinate
There are plenty of tasks in which all can
participate
We have sought many who were
no where to be found
We were about to give up and discovered
you were always around

Many are seeking to get off the ground

What they need is advice which is sound
We wonder where they were when they were
Needed the most
We looked around and discovered they left
Their post

This will add to challenges every day
The load is already too heavy hear what we
say
There were many whom we thought we could
rely on
We truly regret our decisions which
was terribly wrong

IN CONCLUSION I SAY:

Many needs have been neglected far too long
How were we able to rely on those whose tasks
Calls-were neglected far to long
Due to neglect and no considerations for anyone
Today is a new day which has only just begun

Your Past How It Reflects You Today

JUNE 2, 2003

Your past is full of events

Many of which you could not prevent

Man looks at one's past to make decisions

Today

Unfortunately, such events should not

Hinder success along the way

Someone may not be given a chance to advance

Due to past events which happened by chance

A person may have no choice in some events

Tragically success is something which someone

Will try to prevent

This is an obstacle which many will face

Someone will assist while there is space
You will be given a chance
To prosper succeed and advance

One may have made tragic mistakes
In the past
A good future just may be around the
Corner at last
Most believe one should be given a
Second chance
They may have the talent to succeed
And advance

We will open the door for many
Seeking to remove all obstacles if any
We can send them on their way
They can then begin a new life
Any day

There are a lot of jobs which must
Be filled
We will carry out the task according
To Gods will

. . .

Many positions have been vacated
Far too long
As a result, businesses have failed
And things went terribly wrong

Many weren't given a chance
Which hindered their opportunity to
advance
As we said they made a mistake in
their past
It should not hinder opportunities
For a successful future at last

IN CONCLUSION I SAY:

There is a task in which all should
be allowed to serve
we will give them the chance they
deserve
Their talent will benefit many
As they carry out their task without
Neglecting any

A Call Waiting For You

MARCH 14, 2007

There is a call still waiting for you.

Which has potential benefits for only a few.

They have sought help along the way.

Tragically no one heard what they had to say!

Their suffering has led to a crisis affecting not only a few,

but society as a whole, wouldn't come to their aid, which was all familiar.

There may have been opportunities to solve this yesterday,

which would have resulted in prosperity if,

there was no delay.

Some crisis will not be resolved overnight,

We must carefully plan while our budget is tight!

We realize some sacrifices will be tough.
However, there are resources in which we all will get enough!

We will stretch them as far as we can,
in which is a tough message for all to understand!
There is a key role in which to take part,
You must fulfill yours while time is short!

We will seek to carry out an urgent task today,
for benefits to arrive each day.
We pray everyone will do their part and serve the lord!
Bringing an end to our crisis which no one deserves.

There are new tasks arriving every day.
Which brings relief and comfort without delay,
No one can promise crisis in the future will not arrive.
When they occur new tasks will be carried out in which
All must strive.

The crisis we faced yesterday are not
Necessarily a lesson on how to deal
With what we face today
Each day will bring crisis which may be resolved.

One thing we know for certain

Is, there is room for everyone to get involved!

IN CONCLUSION I SAY:

Crisis will certainly arrive any day.

We must cope without delay.

Never seek solutions from the past, but

concentrate on new ones bringing relief at last!

A Challenge At Home

OCT 7, 2003

Challenges here at home are mighty large.
We need many to rise on their feet and take
charge.
There are many tasks which remain unfulfilled.
We will seek someone to carry them out at their
own free will!

Many have suffered enough.
There are tasks to carry out which are tough.
We ask all to seek and carry out their callings,
which will benefit mankind for once and for all!

We must seek assistance from those in need.
This is a call for many to carry out good deeds.

Tomorrow, they can join us in the fight we face.
They will seek calls and be ready to take their
place.

We will proceed and not procrastinate.
Otherwise, many will suffer from what we do
not expect or anticipate.
If you discover one who has a need
send them to us where there is help indeed!

We are saddened by the crisis we see.
There must be a solution on which all
can agree.
What the solution shall be is something for
us to work out.

We expect all to benefit and be given
opportunities beyond a doubt!

We will give all a chance allowing
them to prosper, succeed and advance.
They shall seek to benefit along the way.
Which will give all a chance seeking

a better day!

We expect everyone to benefit from.
our call.
Tomorrow they will seek a call to
prevent a tragic fall.
We will assist them along the way,
listening to them and what those,
whom they will assist will have to say.

IN CONCLUSION I SAY:

We must seek relief from
problems, at home now.
There is someone who
Know the way and will
show us how.
By letting everyone do their part.
Work no matter how or what we start!

A Cry For Help

MARCH 14, 2007

Many sought helps and looked every way
We could not find it until today
Some still suffer from tragic pain
They will quickly recover and seek hope which
carry out
They will gain

We wonder if you specialize in any tasks
dealing
With depression
We need assistance from those full of
suggestion on
Their actions are more than what we can
anticipate

We must act quickly, or it will soon be too late

Many need your help which they tried to seek
We told them you will meet with them next
week
This may be too late for those who suffer the
most
We have located many specialists who are
willing to
Leave their posts

We will have to seek another way
To get you the help you need for a better day
We've located many who are willing to go out
of
Their way
Our response: God bless them we can now
enjoy our day

Many have sent us to you who can fulfill every
need

As a result of the service, we are truly blessed

indeed

You will face a busy task tomorrow

Your talent will relieve many of tragedy,

heartache and

Sorrow

We specialize in helping those in need

With our assistance many will be blessed indeed

We will have the assistance of those who will

sacrifice

There is nothing more we can ask from them

other than

Sound advice

We would love to refer someone to you

Several specialists have made a difference

So, can you

The tasks you carry out will be difficult and

tough

Once the patient recovers, they will respond:

Thank God!

I have enough

IN CONCLUSION I SAY:

. . .

Many tasks for help aren't easy

to carry out

One thing is certain they will truly

benefit beyond a doubt

Who will your task seek to

relieve

In the road to recovery, one must act

On what they truly believe

A Duty To Speak Up

FEB 23, 2004

The one who is weak has critical
needs which they seek!
They don't know the directions in which they
Should go.
They need our assistance which we will show.

They have suffered too long.
They may seek a remedy which was
proven to be wrong.
Have you considered this your call?
It is a great opportunity to benefit many,
who has suffered a tragic fall?

There is a man who is seeking assistance,

who lives down the street,
He is ready to assist the one who he will meet.
Thank God he has not been too busy in the past!
He has pledged to sacrifice for the benefit of many
who has suffered in the past!

We need transportation assistance for those who need
To get around
This is a task which many have found.
Many will sacrifice to get them where they have
to go
They need the directions which we will gladly
show.

As long as the less fortunate are with us,
we have a duty to defend ourselves without a fuss.
We will use the resources which we have today,
to benefit many without unnecessary delay!

What task are you willing to carry out?
Some members are new and must be given
the benefit without the doubt.
We shall act on their behalf and according to Gods will

You may assist in carrying out any task
if you will!

We have a voice which is loud and clear,
to benefit the less fortunate who are nearby.
We will assist them and make a way,
For them to get on their feet without delay.

IN CONCLUSION I SAY:
There are many who need our help and we
will raise our voice,
We have a call without leaving us a choice!
If we do not carry it out, many will suffer.
So, we will raise our voices and shout!

A Favor Is Needed: Can We Rely On You

JAN 7, 2005

Many have burdens which go unmet
To make ends there are goals which we
Must set
We have heard of many challenges with which
You have experience
With your help many can truly make a great
Difference

Many are seeking the opportunity to carry out
Their call
They know they can make a difference after all
They are prepared with priorities set
Together they can achieve goals which must be

set

Have you met one with a critical need unsolved
Send them to us many will get involved
Our call is to assist in any way we can
You have an urgent need which we clearly
understand

We have fulfilled similar needs in the past
Many of whom have benefitted finding
Happiness at last
We hope you will join them today
Tomorrow will truly bring hope for a better day

Many have critical needs which only you can
fulfill
We pray you will carry them out according to
God's will

The challenges you face are mighty tough
However you will need the assistance from
Those who experienced similar challenges

. . .

Which are rough

Have you experienced a situation with which
you
Can't cope
Help is available bringing opportunity and hope
If you need assistance just let us know
We will provide guidance in the direction you
should go

No one should suffer when a call is carried out
Otherwise they weren't given the benefit of a
doubt
Is your call one which will carry out such
A task
We will refer them and assist them when they
ask

IN CONCLUSION I SAY:

We are determined to carry out tasks
Fulfilling critical needs
This is a tough task performing good deeds

We will proceed and not procrastinate

We expect all to benefit before it's too late

A Second Chance To Carry Out Your Call

JAN 14, 2001

Many truly thought the servants were ready to carry out
Their calls
We were left disappointed and suffered a great fall

Everyone had high hopes they wished to achieve
They were tragically misled and viciously deceived

Perhaps the callers had expectations they could not meet
They should have sought help which was right down the
street
Many were convinced the caller could make a great
difference
They were truly disappointed with the experience

. . .

We need one who is bold enough to act
Anyone answering a call must be in a position to
Face tough facts
All calls resulting in benefits will experience tough
challenges
The caller must seek assistance with a tasks they aren't able
to Manage

We wonder if we can rely on the
procrastinator today
Their procrastination is the cause of
tragic delay
We will give them another chance
to carry out their call
They however, will not be allowed
to procrastinate when they
are approached and asked

IN CONCLUSION I SAY:

Procrastination should not be
tolerated in any call
This will only cause delay for the

benefit of all
We will go out of our way
As a sacrifice to benefit mankind
each and every day

Did you find the assistant with talent for the task
You must seek them with questions to ask
Many were available yesterday
They are seeking opportunities each and every day

Have you decided to carry out your call
For the benefit of mankind for once and for all
Many will give you the benefit of a doubt
They are ready to assist in any task which they will
Carry out

We have decided to carry out a task for the benefit of
Mankind
We will search for assistants who are hard to find
Our task will not come to an end
There are principles involved which we truly defend

A Time To Let Go

JUNE 7, 2004

There are challenges which lead the way
Many will go contrary to what we say
You may wish to depart and go your way
This should be the start for a better day

There are many who refuse to cooperate
They insist on their own way and will not
participate
They should advise of the opportunities
which
They should seek
You should depart from their company next
week

. . .

You may avoid them and not get involved
Leave them alone with their own problems
To solve
They should be told where they can seek
advice
We will not get involved, much less make
A sacrifice

We are willing to show you the way
Hoping you will surely have a nice day
We have assistants who will show
You where to go
Because you don't participate, we have
No choice but to let you go

We only desire those who will participate
And assist in our tasks before it's too late
You had a chance before
You failed in your call when we opened
The door

There may be some whom we may
terminate

If they fail in their task while it is late
We will give you one more chance
To prosper succeed-and-given-the
chance to advance

There are many who will carry out
the task
You must be available to assist
whenever
You are asked
We will show you where to go
You will carry out a task which you
Should know

IN CONCLUSION I SAY

We will meet some to whom the answer
will be no
They went contrary to the directions
which we clearly show
You may deal with them one day
Be firm in all you have to say

Acknowledging New Tasks

SEPT 17, 2000

As we unite and acknowledge our needs
We all have to carry out worthy deeds
There are a lot of tasks in which we will all take part
We must be sensitive as we seek where we shall start

You will be accountable for every task
Which you left undone
There is no one to defend you who
resides under the sun

With a deadline to meet there are so many directions
We must not fall short of critical expectations
No one is expected to carry out more than a reasonable
needs

Share

The task they crazy is a clear demonstration on how

They care

No one can hold them accountable of what they don't

Anticipate

There are abundance of tasks in which they participate

They are ready to proceed and not procrastinate

They will fulfill their call before it's too late

IN CONCLUSION I SAY:

Your call is critical in fulfilling our

You should seek help in carrying out the

deeds

Some are too technical for you to carry

Out alone

If you seek the attention of the experts

Everyone will benefit and nothing will

go wrong

We have wrote out a plan which will benefit many

All needs will be fulfilled without neglecting any
Have you fulfilled your task listed in the plan
It is a great one and in serious demand

We will assist you as you seek to carry it out
All will be given the benefit of a doubt
We have discovered that many needs have recently arise
This should not come to any one as a surprise

Answer your call which must be fulfilled today
It is critical to seek opportunities without unreasonable delay
We have fulfilled tasks which were in great demand
Many have benefited by carrying out God's command

We regret that to this day many calls go unfulfilled
Are you one who is guilty of neglecting God's will

An Urgent Call In Time Of Crisis

FEB 2, 2004

We have an urgent call to carry out today
Can you assist us without delay
There are many needs which must be fulfilled
We are determined to carry them out according to
God's will

We replied we are sensitive and truly understand-
We will seek whatever challenges we can perform
This is the first step leading to reform

We will seek the assistance of many with talent
There talent is a great message which God has sent
We will seek their assistance without delay
We will greatly succeed in the role they play

. . .

We will rely on you to do your part
Let us know when you are ready to start
There are many approaching us every day
Without the help we need there will always be
A delay

Calls neglected frequently result in crisis along
The way
The best remedy is to seek tasks today
We ask are any of the tasks part of your call
You should carry them out for the benefit
Of all

Mankind is suffering and has needs which
Must be fulfilled
We will do out best to carry them out according
To God's will
Your call is a difficult one to manage
With our help we will all succeed in the
Challenge

There are tragic situations we face

However there is room for you to
take your place
Neglecting calls result in crisis
which no one deserve
However, the
crisis are critical opportunities for
Many are urging us to assist them in any way we can all
To take their place and-serve

IN CONCLUSION, I SAY:

Crisis are critical times which
allow one to learn
There are benefits and income for
all to carne
Let your call avert another crisis
today
which allows mankind to be
blessed each and every day

Anger Never Gets Everything Right

JUNE 4, 2004

We approached you yesterday and realized

You were upset

We allowed you time to get your priorities set

You cannot proceed with this attitude

We have clients to whom you may seem rude

One of our associates are ready to meet you

Your situation will be a challenge which is new

He has consulted with clients who experienced

Challenges before

However, your situation is new which

May open a door

We specialize in psychology dealing with

Heartache and stress
We believe your task is one which is a difficult
Test
We are determined it is not one which is
Beyond what we can achieve
Yours is a situation out of which one must
Act on faith and belief

Success in dealing with you will be achieved
In time
We have failed in a few tasks which have
Resulted in violent crimes
We do not anticipate this with you
Clients who cooperate fully are only a few

We will seek as many whom we
May assist without delay
The problems are critical and serious
Which they face every day
They deserve a benefit beyond the doubt
Which require technical training no one doubt

The client suffers from pain which they don't

Deserve
They should be given the best treatment by the
One who serves

We will set the highest standards with
Which they must comply
The public can trust us in whom they
Rely

Society is seeking assistance on behalf
of many today
They are searching for remedies without
delay
We ask that you contribute whatever
you can
the problems from which many suffer
clearly speaks for themselves
Which all should understand

IN CONCLUSION I SAY:

Anger will not benefit you any day
We encourage you to seek remedies

which

are available every day

This is the first step for a new start

We encourage you to seek it while time

be short

Approaching Hostle Adversaries

FEB 21, 2000

Yon may think you have something to gain
The evidence will show you caused a lot of pain
You should stick to morality and the good command
You insist on your own way as you demand

We have a lot of work in this place
It must be completed at a fair pace
You must stick to our law principle and reason
Or seek another post this season

Our subordinates are firm on a fair tract
We must use a tough message which is a fact
We are ready for anyone who slips with his foot
He will see a cut in benefits which he thought many

Overlooked

No one will be placed above the law as we start
You think you are tough but proved to be a crook
From the start
Woe to you in the end you will fight a fight which
You just can't win
When we prove our point see who will win

Prior to trusting one desiring a call
Question his intentions for the benefit of all
It is not the will of God that he mislead and offend
This is your chance to fight back and defend

What is your main concern as you proceed to teach
We will assist those whose hands we reach
No one will profit from unjust gain
He has nothing waiting for him but pain

We shall accept the calls of the humble and just to lead
The way
We are willing to follow such leads each and every day
If you have no desire to share and live

Depart from us with your graft,
We believe in one who gives

You call yourself a leader meant to instruct and lead the way
It is time to face reality and proceed without delay
We ask that you refrain from what leads to
Destruction and shame

We have a desire for change and reform
nothing will ever be the same

IN CONCLUSION I SAY:

We seek the leadership of one who is
gentle and kind
He is willing to go out of his way and
sacrifice which he doesn't mind
to have one only with words isn't
the message that God sent
this is the one we all wish to prevent

Avoid False Hope

NOV 6, 2015

You will see friendly faces only once a week
The remaining six days contact with you is what
they will not seek
They pretend and deceive many convincing
them that they Care
It is time to recognize that there isn't a moment
with you they are
Willing to share

You are frequently alone in any task which you
seek to carry out
There is no one among them who is willing to
give you the benefit
Of a doubt

You will rejoice and prosper some day
When they approach you just say have a nice
day

They try to forget how they were in the past
It is a tragic memory which will only last
Who among them ever thought of you
I bet you can't find one who is facing the fact
You are through

Your company is what they won't hang around
God bless them there is one who is true remains
to be found
When they arrive it is time to celebrate
They arrived at last and it isn't too late

There is hope to seek for a better day tomorrow
When it arrives you will be relieved of
heartache and sorrow

It is not a time to remember the past
Thank God for a true one at last

. . .

They will not forsake you when
tough times arrive
They will comfort you while both of
you are alive
They are aware of the heartache which
Took place
They will console you while they remain
faithful and take their Place
Let-this be-a-lesson-while-seeking those
with whom you
Associate
Be patient until the right time comes, it is
never too late
You will know when the moment has
arrived
And enjoy the benefits of which you
won't be deprived

IN CONCLUSION I SAY:

Yon should take time seeking
the right one

. . .

This is a moment has just begun

Try to avoid the one who is out

For only what they can get

If you fell for it you did not take

the time to have priorities set

Avoiding Traps Which We Can't Escape

NOV 6, 2015

There may be situations in which you can't

Fight

Take your time and seek what is right

You may run into a situation which

You don't anticipate

Once you realize it, your actions

May be too late

We are often trapped by those who mean

Us no good

There may be a way for you to escape

Which-you-should

Search for a red flag which

Should be around

There may a path in which to

Escape which you should

Have found

They may seek to trap you from

What you don't see

This is unfortunate and all Someone will seek a trap for those

Agree

Before you fall seek advice which

Is sound

The advisor is near and easy to be

Found

When something looks good take

Time to investigate

Or you will suffer consequences and

It will be too late

Even the court may not be able to

Come to your defense

When approaching something un-

Familiar be alert and full of suspense

Victims are often trapped by crooks every day

Seek a plan which will result in their
Delay
Be careful when letting them know
When you are in doubt
The task should be theirs to take time

And figure it out

This may slow down the crooked
games they play
Which is to your advantage to seek
Another way
They will soon figure out a clue
They clearly made a mistake running
into someone who is as smart as you

Observe clues when they are around
the crook will know the one who is
wise and sound
they realize you are too smart for
their game
They will seek other victims who
clearly don't think the same

. . .

IN CONCLUSION I SAY:

who are easily deceived

This is a tragic teaching which

All should receive

They seek games to prey on those

who are weak

We will truly seek to bring them to

Justice this week

Beware Of Red Flags

FEB 25, 2004

Beware of red flags which are brought
To your attention
The matter is serious which one hasn't
Mentioned
The person may not have had a
Fraudulent intent
You were taught to spot them from
Wherever they were sent

We must recognize a situation which
The system will reject
We shall correct the laymen with all
Due respect
They should be given the benefit of a doubt

They are left with problems to figure out

We must assist them in any way we can
Our goal is that they will fully understand
They will seek advice on which they can rely
There are rules with which all must comply

You hold a position which the layman has
Never held before
He expects your assistance as he arrives
At the door
He will have many questions to ask
Answering them and providing guidance
Is your task

Technology will create systems which will
Be in high demand
You will be trained and guided so you will
Understand
The layman will rely on you to show him
The way

You will have a task which starts today

. . .

Red flags may be difficult for the
Layman to see
He may not have the fraudulent intent on
which
All-ean-agree
You are trained to recognize them on the spot

With your experience you truly
should have
Seen a Iot
We have a duty to recognize a
problem on the spot
we have corrected a mistake which
were a lot
We must protect the layman from
Trouble
which they may find
this is a task for us to carry out and
we truly don't mind

IN CONCLUSION I SAY:
We have a duty which must be
carried out

Everyone is given the benefit of

a doubt

Red flags must be recognized without

Delay

Dealing with them in our task each

And every day

Be Aware Of The Task Before You Ask

FEB 1, 2004

There are tasks in which we are all involved

There are crisis which must be solved

Will you fulfill the need

The challenges are truly tough in deed

You have a call to carry out

Many will truly benefit without a doubt

You will need assistance along the way

Take time and seek it without delay

Some tasks seem more simple than what they

are

If the wrong person seeks the task they won't get

very far

This will delay benefits any day
Another crisis will be coming along the way

We must put the right person in charge
The task they face is truly large
Their experience have proven they are right for
the task
They are available whenever they are asked

We will seek them wherever they can be found
So far we have looked and they were nowhere
around
Thank God someone located them yesterday
We can now relax throughout the day

They are happy to take on the task
They need out assistance and have already asked
The challenges are tough which they must face
There is room for all assistants to take their
place

We ask that you be patient in carrying out your
call

For the benefit of mankind for once and for all
We need everyone to faithfully carry out their
task
Many needs will be fulfilled on behalf of those
who ask

IN CONCLUSION I SAY:

There are many tasks involved in a great
challenge
We must seek the one who can successfully
manage
He has proven this by experience in the past
Many have testified he has blessed so many at
last

Calls Neglected Create Opportunities

JUNE 18, 2012

Many have neglected opportunities which will
Truly benefit mankind
Let us proceed with whom we will find
There were tasks which weren't carried out
As a result many weren't given the benefit
Of a doubt

We all have a call to carry out and
Serve
You should serve man giving him the benefit which he
Richly deserves
Tragically many have failed in the tasks of their
Calls

We will seek to benefit many for once and for all

There are many with talent whom we will
Seek
They are ready to proceed starting next week
We regret many are suffering today
Their call will benefit all without delay

We will not be able to fulfill the tasks alone
Those who proceeded us have tried this
Which resulted in things going terribly wrong
We ask that you assist us in the tasks to be
Carried out
We are certain that many will benefit which no one
Can doubt

We will seek to do what we can
We request that you be patient and understand
We have been approached by many regarding the
Problems they face
This creates a heavy demand on those
Who serve as we all take our place

. . .

We have a long list regarding many needs
We week to carry out the tasks fulfilling good
Deeds
We pray all needs are fulfilled which are listed
Above
We seek God's help and can't proceed without
His unconditional love

Our tasks will assist many in each and
Every way
We will seek your assistance along the way

The day will come when you will carry
out your call
Which is expected to benefit man for
once and for all

IN CONCLUSION I SAY:

Your call should be carried out without
delay
If you can't fulfill it please step aside
and make away

We are determined to see that all tasks

are faithfully carried out

And benefit mankind which no one can

doubt

Challenges Are Involved In Everything We Do

MAY, 20 2016

Every call which is meant to benefit man will
have a variety of challenges
The call will be called out by one who is
competent to manage
We have suffered due to calls not being carried
out
As you seek a challenge we will give you the
benefit of a doubt

Everyone will seek a call which will benefit
many in some way
Those who will benefit cannot tolerate
procrastination along the way
There are people who sought calls yesterday

Unfortunately, they suffered a terrible setback
Due to procrastination and a failure to act
without delay

We urge you to proceed which will give many
the benefit they deserve
Tomorrow they will seek a call which is a
challenge to carry out and serve
Your call will result in many being blessed
This is an opportunity allowing all to do their
best

Nover be discourage when a challenge comes
your way
Be prepared to face them any day
Your challenge involves many tasks in which
you must do your part
The task you carry out involves many
opportunities for us to finish the task
We start

We all have a desire to do what we can
In every call, we must carry out every task

which is in great demand
We all desire to be blessed with call of a great
challenge
Our success is determined in how well we
manage

Challenges will come when time brings about a
change
They are top priorities which we will arrange
The challenges we face are great
The task will be carried out before it's too late

We have suffered due to calls being neglected
for various reasons
We are prepared for a change every season
Many will recover from a tragic fall
Once they do they are prepared for a great call

Challenges are what make a call great
You should carry out yours before it's too late
Your call should provide opportunities for relief
Many will be relived from pain suffering and
grief

. . .

IN CONCLUSION I SAY:

This is the day for you to seek a

Challenge

yours is the one which you have

The gift to manage

many suffered until they found you

Now is the time to see what you can do.

Challenges To Srengthen Us

MARCH 3, 2007

We all seek challenges which are tough
They require decisions which are tough
They seek to strengthen us every day
We must use caution and not go astray

There is a task for you today
It is a tough call which must be answered without
Delay
Your call will solve many needs
You will be required to carty out tough deeds

We have witnessed many tragedies in the past
Which created calls which must be carried out at
last

Crisis will arise when someone neglect their call
This is a tragedy we hope to end for once and for
all

If you know someone who has neglected a call in
the past
Send them to us we have remedies which will be
tough and
Meant to last
We will not tolerate procrastination any day
If you don't proceed, we will send you away

Your challenge is measured by your strengthen
and determination
The task you carry out depends on the current
situation
The crisis we face are a challenge indeed
They provide opportunities to fulfill many needs

We will seek to fulfill every task we can
We will seek the assistance of those who
understand
We are sensitive to those who are suffering

today

We will sacrifice and assist.them.cach.and

every day

We will assist them in every call which they

seek to carry out

Their call will benefit everyone which no

one can doubt

They have a need which only you can fulfill

You should carry it out today according to

God's will

IN CONCLUSION I SAY:

We welcome the challenge in which

everyone is involved

There are problems which will take time to

solve

Be patient you will experience relief

tomorrow

Which will end all heartache grief and

Sorrow

Challenging Authority

JUNE 2, 2003

You must hold those who are in charge
To a higher standard when carrying out
Tasks which are large
They may be human like the rest of us
We will assist them as we prepare and travel by bus

We have a task to assist as long as they carry out
Their duties according to the law
We will carry out every task which is not forbidden
By law
There are many whose task it is to assist along the
way
We must stay on track without going astray

. . .

Tragically many will fall short of what we expect
They will fall in disgrace losing all respect
Hopefully they have committed no crime
If so they must prepare for a sentence and serve
time

Those in high places are not above the law
They are clearly headed for what they truly saw
They shall be brought to justice like the rest
Of us
We are ready to carry it out without a great
Fuss

We clearly say the position to which you were
elected
Which Is one we greatly respect
Your disgrace and sin is a shame
Once you are removed things won't be
The same

We seek those who demand high respect
Your position is one in which you must
carry out tasks

we respect
Your acts have led to a tragic fall
As a result we will file papers to have
you recalled

Your case will then be sent to the court
There are documents which we will sort
If prosecuting is justified then it should be
Carried out
We will then assist them which no one
can doubt

IN CONCLUSION I SAY:

Those in high positions will be held
to high
standards which-we-all-truly-respect-
They will execute tasks and not fall short
Of what the public expects
If you have a problem with your duties
to perform
You should not seek reelection
this is a chance for reform

Confronting Adversaries

JAN 5, 2010

You will frequently work with people who do not view
Things your way
Take time to hear what they have to say
Their point of view just may be right
Which is what you did not consider last night

The truth will come out for all to hear
Once it does no one will have anything to fear
There will be conflicts which must be solved
This is an opportunity for all to participate and get
Involved

The conflicts we deal with are not new
The solutions to solve them are only a few

You may have a different point of view
I have solutions which many may wish to review

We have seen conflicts which were solved in the past
Some came up with many solutions which were meant to
Last
Many had to carry out difficult tasks
Those with a different point of view were glad to assist
When asked

We will seek the opinions of those who meet with us
We will greet them when they arrive by bus
They have taught us a lot which we did not expect
To hear
We will seek to work with them without hostility
Or fear

We were informed of conflicts which we may face
We will proceed with everyone taking their place
We will start by listening to your point of view
The group will consider it and proceed to review

The public has expressed an interest in what all have to say

They will be invited to take part without delay
Hopefully someone will come up with a solution
While there is time
The taxpayer will not have to spend another dime

IN CONCLUSION I SAY:

We will solve conflicts in a
peaceful way
They will be invited to take
part without delay
Hopefully we will end our
conflicts tomorrow
Which will possibly leave
no room for pain heartache
or sorrow

Coping With Frustration

JAN 14, 2001

There are tasks which will result in frustration
You may experience it in any situation
This is a task with which all must cope
Try to look beyond it while there is hope

If you are not careful it just may ruin your health
Destroying all opportunities for possible success and wealth
There is no excuse for opportunities to be missed today
Which will only deprive us of benefits
We should enjoy any day

We have an obligation to assist who we can
Which involves tough tasks we truly understand
The first step is to seek the care you need

You will then be well enough to carry out the deed

Many are not well enough to carry out their tasks
Tomorrow
We are all grieved and struck with sorrow
Frustration is a task which all must overcome
We will be able to benefit many and then some

Frustration will no longer get us down
We will seek advice which is clear and sound
Many are available who specialize in these tasks
Once they are found they will perform favors when asked

We seek to get many on their feet
And overcome all obstacles which they may meet
They will have their priorities set
They will carry out tasks in which needs will be met

They must first seek the help they need
Which involves carrying out tough tasks indeed
Is your call one which is in high demand
You will need assistance which we all understand

. . .

In conclusion I say:

We must not be defeated in the obstacle of frustration
However, we will experience it in a lot of situations
Coping with it is a tough daily task
Help is available for all who ask

Corruption That Will Wake You Up

SEPT 29, 2008

In your daily life, you may witness what you do not desire.

You should seek to make a change and enjoy what you aspire.

The graph of the crooked will come to light.

There has never come a better time for us to fight.

We must not fail to be prepared and organized.

While we were sleeping, they took notice and recognized us.

We must use our strength and observe.

When they see us alert, they know they have no reserve.

We must use our voice and speak.

As time goes by, they will surely grow weak.

They will notice they are headed for defeat.

The crook builds hope on a plan which no decent person can.

Stand

At the end of his journey, he discovers that there is a high authority.

Which is in command?

When we rest, he seeks evil deeds not far from hand.

When called on to give an account he will surely suffer as justice demands?

Take notice of corrupt activities in life

It is our duty to fight them without hatred or strife,

Corruption truly contributes to moral delinquency, a sad fact.

We must face it,

A life of stem principle produces benefits putting all in their place.

Be careful in all choices which you make.

Many may be influenced by the choice you make.

Those who rely on you expect what is right.

Keep this in mind, stand on guard and be ready to

Fight

We stand behind those who are ready to lead.

We have witnessed their plan for all to succeed.

You will have your chance tomorrow.

When you carry your call without sorrow

. . .

IN CONCLUSION I SAY:

We must all avoid corruption no matter what the cost.

Or else we set up disaster and what a wonderful opportunity.

We have lost.

Mankind is relying on you to carry out your call today.

As a result of this he can hope

for a better day

JUNE 13, 2004

We are happy you answered your call
Many were suffering and are relieved
After all
We thank God we located you yesterday
You carried out the task without delay

The crisis from which we suffered has
created a call for you
Unfortunately, the tasks are many but the
servants
Who act-are only-a-few
We need many who will answer their call
Until they do we may not be be able to

prevent a tragic fall

You should try to get others involved
There are problems which they have the
talent to solve
There is room to recruit many along the way
Hopefully they will seek their call without
delay

We pray the crisis we face will soon come to
an end
As long as a call is neglected we must assist
those whom we defend
The pain from which they suffer is tragic
and sad
The one whom they relied on is no longer
around whom they called dad

We are determined that we should go out of
Our way
They shall soon rise on their feet seeking a
Better day

. . .

They are assisted as long as there is a need
We truly expect them to do their part indeed

Our question is when will you proceed and
carry out your call
There are many who rely on you and they
are right down the hall
You don't have to look far away
They will be at a location where you will
find them today

We must assist everyone who seeks a call
There are benefits which they can fulfill
after all
There are resources which we have to go
around
We urge you to seek them while they can be
found

IN CONCLUSION I SAY:

We can prevent tragic crisis anytime
If we proceed they won't cost us a dime

There are calls which aren't fulfilled

Someone has neglected to carry out God's

will

Crisis: A Challenge For Every Call

JUNE 15, 2004

Are you prepared for the challenges of
Your call
They should be faithfully carried out to
Prevent a tragic fall
We have witnessed many in the past
The challenge of your call should
Prevent them at last

Many who suffered have recovered from
Heartache and pain
They have sought opportunities from which all have gained
They carried out a task with you in mind
They-will-be-generous-and-perform-acts-which

Are kind

We will assist those who seek relief today
We are prepared to sacrifice and go out
Of our way
They should not let anyone suffer alone
Leaving them to fend for themselves is truly
Unkind and wrong

There are calls to prevent acts of this kind
Such calls should be carried out by those
Who don't mind
We were disappointed when
We found only a few
Now we face a new challenge
As we approach you

We have witnessed more tragic facts than what
We can handle alone
There is so much tragic abuse which is wrong
We have the resources to carry out the deed
The challenge we face is intense to find those
Who are willing to serve in deed

. . .

The crisis we currently face could have
Been prevented if one acted soon enough
This creates a challenge before us which
Is tough
We can only predict what the end will be
When the time arrives, it is an event
Which all will witness and see
We will carry out every challenge which has
been neglected in the past
there are calls for all to seek are you seeking
One resulting in relief at last
The road to recovery is not too far away
It will soon approach if you seek a task today

IN CONCLUSION I SAY:

The-crisis which-we-currently
face has a task for all
If faithfully carried out there are
benefits for one and all
We will proceed on the day
coming to an end
Before we complete the task we

will wonder

How many have we

Successfully and defended

Crisis Demand That Tough Choices Be Carried Out

JUNE 18, 2002

Without a doubt your call will demand a tough choice
What you need is a loud and clear voice
The decision will be a tough one to make
It will keep many on their feet for their own sake

Every call will face crisis along the way
You must be prepared as you start your day
Crisis will arise as none of us expect
Calls in crisis will earn one great respect

None of us anticipate the crises we will face
While dealing with them.an urgent.call.is to take-your-place-
Be prepared to come with decisions which are wise

They surely won't come to one as a surprise

Crisis tragically result from calls neglected
Someone was negligent in the one whom they have selected
They may have had good intentions which no one will doubt
However they must be held accountable and justice will be carried out

Good intentions aren't good enough
Justice must prevail which is tough
What the person did not intend is the harm they have caused
Justice must be sought while many are still and pause

You may not anticipate a crisis as you carry out your task
Keep in mind you are never too smart to seek advice and ask
Crisis are tough moments which none of us deserve
You are nevertheless are urged to carry out your call and serve

You should seek high standards with every client who seeks relief
Such standards may bring an end to suffering sadness and grief
Many specialists will offer assistance without delay
Can they truly rely on you one day

. . .

IN CONCLUSION I SAY:

Have you faced a crisis in your call

Help is available for one and all

The help you seek is critical today

You should seek it immediate while it is available any day

Crisis: Many Calls Are In Demand

NOV 22, 2004

Crisis are a time of trouble in which many

Must get involved

There are problems which we must solve

There may be a shortage of help which we expected

We however will not come up short of what anyone expected

These are tough times in which all must take part

There are time limits for all to do their part

No one should fall short along the way

If you need assistance help is available any day

Moments of crisis are times in which everyone should

Sacrifice

Help is available when seeking advice

Take time to seek it when in need

This will lead to success and prosperity
In deed

Crisis are opportunities for all to seek
A call
Your call can be a benefit for once and
for all
You should seek opportunities this week
Just remember to stay humble and meek

The crisis which took place may lead to another direction
We will seek advice and many suggestions
The time for recovery may be near
We will abide by your advice which is loud and clear

Crisis frequently result when advice is overlooked
There were opportunities where many should have looked
There are opportunities in which all must participate
Time limits forbid anyone should procrastinate

If you are ready just let us know

We will advise you of the directions in which
You should go
Help is available in the direction you seek
While seeking it just remember to stay
Humble and meek

IN CONCLUSION I SAY:

Crisis are a critical opportunity for all to
learn
This is a critical time for respect
to be earned
The opportunity is
is available every day
you will be blessed to seek it
without delay

Crisis: What Opportunities Do They Provide

OCT 3, 2003

Crisis provide opportunities for you to carry out your call
There should be a task carried out for the benefit of all
Have you sought the one meant for you
There should be rewards for many not just a few

Many have sought the help they need
They seek the one who will carry out the deed
There are many calls which we are determined to carry out
Let those who will sacrifice go out of their way which no one
Can doubt

We are determined that no one should miss the blessing-they-
Seek
Which will demand that we carry out many tasks this week

Many have suffered which they don't deserve
Which is a sign that many went astray when they should
Have served

Can they rely on you in time of need
Many can only wonder who will carry out the deed
If you are not available any day we suggest that you step
Aside and make a way

You have been a stumbling block in the past
We will no longer tolerate this and will this and we
Will proceed mighty fast
We regret that many have not enjoyed the blessing they
Need
Due to the selfishness of those who satisfied their greed

This is what we wish to prevent
We seek the help of the one whom God has sent
If you are not the one, the time has arrived for you to get
Out of the way
Mankind will truly enjoy a better day

We do not need a stumbling block

If you are not the one to fulfill the need

We ask that you vacate the position and the

Door will be locked

There are obstacles which we wish to overcome

We will then enjoy benefits and then some

Crisis: Your Call Is The One For Relief

JUNE 15, 2004

There is a call for you to take the lead
Which will truly relieve many from crisis in deed
We will assist you as we take our place
We should proceed while there is space

We are happy to see a call carried out by you
We regret that the leads we have are slow and
Only a few
This only multiplies the crisis we have at hand
This is a crisis itself which we hope you will
Understand

We were approached by many who
Desires that calls be carried out

They expressed a desire to benefit many which
No one can doubt
They have discussed with us the duties of
Their call
While we were patient and listened we were
Impressed after all

We believe their call is one which is in need
They are ready to carry out the deeds
They will need assistance along the way
This will result in calls being fulfilled without
Delay

We will seek the one who will carry them out
Many will seek relief which no one can doubt
If your call is one which will be carried out today
We truly wish to know if we should wait
Or take the time to seek another way

We will not tolerate one who procrastinates
We are fulfilling needs while many have waited
And it was pretty late
There is an obstacle which we not allow to hold

Anyone back
We are determined to keep all on frack

If you are not ready to proceed please step aside
And make a way
There are many who are ready to
Proceed without delay
Our crisis will end with the fulfillment of
Many calls
Which will benefit many for once and for all

IN CONCLUSION I SAY:

Your call has brought assistance
in relief
You have acted out of concern
and your belief
we wish many would carry out
a similar call
there can be no greater demand
to prevent a tragic fall

Does Your Call Recognize Talent

JUNE 13, 2004

There are many who carry out their talent
This is a clear message which God has sent
You have a call to perform and recognize
This should not come to anyone as a surprise

A lot of people are not given the credit they are due
A lot express envy and strife, what about you
Those with talent should be given the benefit of a doubt
It is a call which your talent will allow you to carry out

You know many with talent have been tragically overlooked
In spite of this they sought every opportunity which they took
This type of neglect will soon come to an end

Or calls may be neglected by those whose duty it is to defend

Have you seen one with talent which you failed to recognize
This should be seen as a tragic surprise
Many may be discouraged from carrying out their call
Due to not being recognized and neglected by all

We seek those who will carry out calls without delay
They will be given respect which is due today
There is a need for help which they will seek
From those whose duty it is to stay humble and meek

Those with such a commitment are only a few
We will seek others who are new
Those with talent need someone who truly understand
And will be around whenever there is a need for a helping
Hand

You will support them in their tasks
You pledged to give assistance whenever you are asked
Today is the day they are truly in need
They will be grateful and thank you for assistance in deed

. . .

IN CONCLUSION I SAY:

We must take the time to recognize those with talent
Many don't recognize it is a gift which God has sent
Can they rely on you to give credit to whom it is due
Many have tragically failed, what about you

Experience Fulfilling Needs

NOV 6, 2015

Your talent will allow you to carry out tasks demanding
Experience
This will truly make a great difference
You will carry out tasks which aren't new
Those who experienced similar tasks before you
Are only a few

Your experience will provide opportunities for
Many to seek
They are ready to start and can't wait until next week

Many have sought to make a difference
Once they were given the opportunity we

Found out that they lack the experience

We were headed for failure until we heard about you
We quickly approached you which allowed us to
Overcome what we went through
It was an unfortunate experience which we had in
The past
Thank God we overcame what we were short of
Which did not last

We will experience a task which is new
Those assisting us will only be a few
We will carry out a task to benefit
Mankind
We ask that you play your part if you don't
Mind

Many unfortunately experience tragedies everyday
We hope our tasks will benefit them as they
Seek a way
To overcome the tragedies which they have experienced
Thank God we can all make a great difference

. . .

We will seek opportunities of every kind
A tragedy provides a call to carry out which we
Truly don't mind
Today is a good day to start a task
Can you proceed while time is short
Which all we ask

We will provide the resources which you will need
They will allow you to fulfill the tasks in deed
We are determined to fulfill human needs of

Calls for these tasks are to be
carried out and we surely don't
mind

IN CONCLUSION I SAY:

Every call is out
is meant to make a difference
We have been told you have the
Experience
many will benefit and seek
opportunities today

they will proceed to benefit

Other without delay

Giving Praise To Whom It Is Due

NOV 6, 2015

Your love has been so gentle and
Mighty strong
That I may profit and suffer no wrong
You have always been available and
Made a way
That I may have a good life each and
Every day

You have been talent and faithful in
All of your teachings
I have the honor of those in whom
Lam reaching
I have been so blessed to have
A loved one like you

You have provided a tough road
For me to get through

You have fought well to the end
Because of you I have a new life
Which today I begin
You have done well in the life
You live
I hope to prosper and have a lot
Which I may give

As I advance, I am aware that many
Are left behind
They truly can advance with acts
Which are so kind
They deserve a chance to succeed
Like us
They must be willing to sacrifice
And endure hardships without
A fuss

We must not forget we were once
Like them before

We have sought opportunities

Which have opened the door

We were assisted with our priorities

Se

This is the first step in reaching

The goals we have met

There is still a lot for us to achieve

We will accomplish this by acting

On the advice we receive

You to can be a success if you act without

delay

There is a lot of work to fulfilled cach and

every day

You must not forget about those who are left

Behind

we ask that you fulfill your task

If you don't mind

They will pursue plenty of opportunities which

they will seek

Tomorrow is not promised much less next

weęk

IN CONCLUSION I SAY:

You have a chance to succeed in everything
you do
Many have fulfilled their task what about you
You said you seek to make a difference
When you carry out your tasks
Many will enjoy a new experience

Untitled

GOD'S GIFT: YOU DID NOT EARN IT

Author: Cheryl Reynolds

Date: Nov 6, 2015

I seek the gift which I did not earn
Which is right in seeking wisdom form
Which we all can learn
The people who benefit will have
A lot to say
Help from God will show all the way

We all need a help in hand
God has a desire for us to carry out all
commands
While many are suffering who will

Carry out the deeds
God will use someone to fulfill all
Of our needs

We will serve with compassion while
Seeking reform
Do you have a sincere desire for a.
Task which must be performed
The people desire benefits for once and
For all
Help me O Lord, I must carry out
My call

There are a lot of gifts which aren't
Carried out according to God's will
We must assist those who are determined
To see that they are fulfilled
The tasks must be fulfilled in a
Matter of time
While we are waiting we have witnessed
A serious crime

Mankind faces a crisis while dealing with
Stress

He has needs which must be addressed

We will assist him while he experiences
A desire for a change
We will assist in priorities which must be
Arranged

We have experienced tasks which were
Difficult to manage
It was an honor to carry out such a
Great challenge
We will carry out every challenge
On behalf of those who ask
We will need God's assistance to carry out our
ţasks
Man suffered due to deeds not carried out
they had heavy burden in which no one gave
them the benefit of a doubt

they have heavy burdens as their daily needs
multiply
we must produce the resources on which they
rely

IN CONCULSION ISAY:

God has a desire to use you for the task which
are to be carried out

We will assist in giving you the benefit beyond

A doubt

Keep in mind that your gift is one which you did

not earn

It should be used to allow him to succeed

prosper and earn

God's Great Plan

DEC 11, 2015

God created a plan from the moment of our birth
Which was the creation of Heaven and Earth
While the Earth was void and without form
Otherwise he may have been in a state of alarm

He would ask for light which was about to appear
He would be able to move around without fear
Many have sought the dream they wish to achieve
It is full of tasks which they truly conceive

They tried to carry out the tasks in the past
Which resulted in mistakes which many hoped
wouldn't
Last

Many have called on you today
To assist in any task without delay
There are calis which all should pursue and seek
Many have suffered heartache and pain during
the week
Many have truly suffered, which they don't
deserve
Many could have prevented this if they carried
out their call and served

If you need assistance just let us know
We are glad to guide you in the direction you
Should go

Many have requested that you send those
Who Seek relief
We can't proceed while we suffer from
pain and grief

We are hindered from carrying out our
tasks
Our burdens will only multiply with
whomever we

Assist once they ask
This is a sever crisis which demand
many calls
We pray someone will understand our
needs for once and for all

We will proceed while the hour is late
We are grieved many are suffering
while others procrastinate
We will seek assistance from those
with experience
As we proceed we know all will
experience a great difference

IN CONCLUSION ISAY:

Many calls tragically go unfulfilled
In spite of this we are determined
carry out God's will

We ask that you carry one this week
Which will truly result in benefits
Many will seek

www.ingramcontent.com/pod-product-compliance
Lightning Source LLC
LaVergne TN
LVHW010546160826
845677LV00013B/3017

* 9 7 9 8 8 9 5 6 9 6 5 8 3 *